A BANK STREET MUSEUM BOOK

DINOSAURIUM

By Barbara Brenner • Illustrated by Donna Braginetz

With an introduction by Dr. Peter Dodson, Science Consultant

To Mark, in memory of dinosaur days.
— B.B.

DINOSAURIUM
A Bantam Book/March 1993

Series graphic design by Alex Jay/Studio J
Senior Editor: Sarah Feldman
Assistant Editor: Kathy Huck
Special thanks to Betsy Gould, William H. Hooks, Hope Innelli,
James A. Levine, and Howard Zimmerman.

Library of Congress Cataloging-in-Publication Data

Brenner, Barbara.
Dinosaurium/by Barbara Brenner;
illustrated by Donna Braginetz.
p.   cm — (Bank Street museum book)
"A Byron Preiss book."
Summary: Describes a museum tour through
the Triassic, Jurassic, and Cretaceous periods
with information about the names and habits
of the dinosaurs. Includes questions
for the reader to answer.
ISBN 0-553-07614-0.   — ISBN 0-553-35427-2 (pbk.)
1. Dinosaurs — Juvenile literature.   [1. Dinosaurs.]
I. Braginetz, Donna, ill.   II. Title   III. Series.
QE862.D5B67   1992
567.91 — dc20
91-6335
CIP
AC

Published simultaneously in the United States and Canada

Bantam Books are published by Bantam Books, a division of Bantam Doubleday Dell Publishing
Group, Inc. Its trademark, consisting of the words "Bantam Books" and the portrayal of a rooster,
is Registered in U.S. Patent and Trademark Office and in other countries. Marca Registrada.
Bantam Books, 666 Fifth Avenue, New York, New York 10103.

PRINTED IN THE UNITED STATES OF AMERICA

0 9 8 7 6 5 4 3 2

Introduction

Dinosaurs are just great. I loved them when I was a kid, and I never outgrew them. Now as a scientist (paleontologist) I study and write about them.

Why should we worry about animals that lived so long ago? Well, they were exotic, beautiful, sometimes terrifying, but they were also real. To learn about dinosaurs is to learn about science, just as to study bean plants growing in paper cups or to look at stars through a telescope is to learn about science. There are so many wonderful facts to learn: *Deinonychus* means "terrible claw"; *Diplodocus* was ninety feet long; *Maiasaura* cared for its young at the nest. But science is not just a set of *facts* that we memorize from books, it is a *process* by which we learn. Knowledge is never static – it is changing all the time. When I was a kid I had never heard of *Deinonychus* or *Maiasaura* because they hadn't been discovered yet. People mainly thought that dinosaurs were dumb and slow moving. Today we know about many more kinds of dinosaurs, because new finds are being made all the time in China, Mongolia, Argentina, Antarctica, as well as Canada and the United States. We now believe that certain dinosaurs were smart and fast moving. New discoveries show that at least one species of dinosaur cared for its young, that some dinosaurs lived near both the north and south poles, and that other dinosaurs migrated long distances.

Discoveries in the years to come will bring new and clearer ideas about how and where the dinosaurs lived. Who knows how your discoveries will better our understanding of dinosaurs if you too decide to become a paleontologist?

Dr. Peter Dodson
Associate Professor of Anatomy
Department of Animal Biology
University of Pennsylvania

ERA	AGE	MILLION YEARS AGO
	Quaternary	
CENOZOIC Mammals evolve		2 Today **People on Earth**
	Tertiary	
		65
MESOZOIC The time of the dinosaurs	Cretaceous	
		145
	Jurassic	
		208
	Triassic	245
PALEOZOIC Life forms evolve on land and sea	Permian	
		286
	Carboniferous	
		360
	Devonian	
		408
	Silurian	438
	Ordovician	
		505
	Cambrian	
		590

Welcome to
the Dinosaurium.
Take a giant step
back in time and
walk with the
dinosaurs into...

THE WORLD OF THE MESOZOIC ERA

MUSEUM PLAN

✖ YOU ARE HERE

THE WORLD OF THE MESOZOIC ERA PAGES 6–9

TIME GARDEN PAGES 10–11

HALL OF AGES CRETACEOUS PAGES 16–17

HALL OF AGES JURASSIC PAGES 14–15

HALL OF AGES TRIASSIC PAGES 12–13

HALL OF WEIGHTS PAGES 18–19

HALL OF BONES PAGES 20–21

DINOSAUR CORRAL PAGES 22–23

FOSSIL LAB PAGES 24–27

HALL OF ARMOR PAGES 34–37

HALL OF FEEDING PAGES 30–33

HALL OF HEADS PAGES 28–29

DINOSAUR NURSERY PAGES 38–39

FLIGHT CHAMBER PAGES 40–41

CAVE OF WONDERS PAGES 42–43

HALL OF FAME PAGES 44–45

About 225 million years ago the very first dinosaurs appeared. They roamed the earth for roughly 160 million years. Hundreds of different species evolved; about 340 of them have been discovered so far.

There were no people alive at the time of the dinosaurs. Everything we know about dinosaurs comes from clues they left: fossil bones and teeth, eggs, skeletons, fossil plants, and...dinosaur tracks.

Look! Dinosaur tracks!

Learning about dinosaurs is probably the world's longest-running mystery and detective game. Sometimes the trails have led nowhere. Other times they've led to the discovery of a totally new dinosaur species. But you don't have to be a scientist to play. Some of the greatest dinosaur discoveries have been made by people—young and old—who just love dinosaurs.

Want to join the great dinosaur hunt? All you have to do is keep your eyes open as you move through the Dinosaurium.

Fossils are the remains of a living thing from a former age.

A fossilized bone.

A fossilized fern.

Here are some scientists looking for clues. What do you suppose they're going to find?

These tracks are one of the mysteries. As you move through the halls, try to figure out what kind of dinosaur made the tracks. Clue: It's one of the first dinosaurs ever discovered.

You are now in the Time Garden. The dinosaurs lived during three time periods of the Mesozoic Era: the Triassic, the Jurassic, and the Cretaceous. They were on the earth for about 160 million years.

Dinosaur evidence has been found in every part of the world. At first people thought dinosaur fossils were the bones of giants. Then, early in the nineteenth century, scientists began to understand that the bones belonged to ancient reptiles.

TIME GARDEN

Brachiosaurus

Apatosaurus

Tyrannosaurus rex

Saltasaurus

Albertosaurus

Ornithomimus

Allosaurus   Deinonychus

Dilophosaurus

Ceratosaurus

Massospondylus

Anchisaurus

Plateosaurus

SAURISCHIAN
(LIZARD-HIPPED)
DINOSAURS

Coelophysis

	MESOZOIC			CENOZOIC
	Triassic	Jurassic	Cretaceous	Present Day
245 Million Years Ago	208 Million Years Ago	145 Million Years Ago	65 Million Years Ago	

The layer of earth in which fossils are found is a clue to when a creature lived. The oldest fossils are usually near the bottom layers of earth.

The early dinosaurs of the Triassic Period were mostly less than ten feet long. In the Jurassic Period there were giant dinosaurs. And by the late Cretaceous Period, there were dinosaurs of every description. Some dinosaurs were as big as a blue whale—the largest living creature in the world today.

Shantungosaurus

Triceratops

Hadrosaurus

Lambeosaurus

Euoplocephalus

Tenontosaurus

Styracosaurus

Camptosaurus

Stegosaurus

Kentrosaurus

Scelidosaurus

Lesothosaurus

ORNITHISCHIAN (BIRD-HIPPED) DINOSAURS

The scientists seem to have found some bones.

Pisanosaurus

These tracks were found in a layer of earth from about 100 million years ago.

11

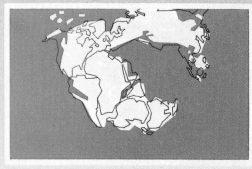

This is how the world looked during the Triassic Period.

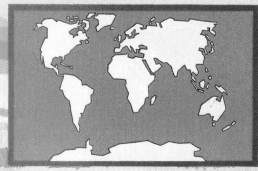

This is how the world looks now.

You're now standing somewhere in the Triassic Period, which began about 245 million years ago. Notice that the weather is dry and not very cold. The land is low; there are plains, deserts, swamps, and forests. In this spot, as elsewhere, there are plants, fish, insects, reptiles, and amphibians. The first dinosaurs and the first tiny mammals have already appeared. These early dinosaurs will travel to every part of the globe.

Eudimorphodon
(Pterosaur)

Plateosaurus

Desmatosuchus
(Aëtosaur)

Rutiodon
(Phytosaur)

HALL OF AGES
TRIASSIC
245–208 MILLION YEARS AGO

THIS WAY TO
THE JURASSIC
→

Placerias
(Dicynodont)

Coelophysis

Could this be
a leg bone?

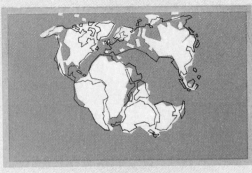

This is how the world looked during the Jurassic Period.

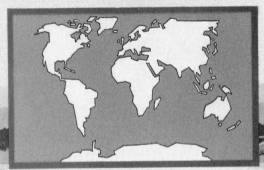

This is how the world looks now.

You have moved into the Jurassic Period. You're on land, but enormous areas of the earth are now covered by water. The Atlantic Ocean is starting to come between Africa and North America. The air is beginning to feel warm and humid like Florida. There are salamanders and a number of different frogs and lizards. Small mammals live on the forest floor. There are flying reptiles as well as dinosaurs. This age is famous for large herds of giant plant-eating dinosaurs.

Diplodocus

Archaeopteryx
(Bird)

Allosaurus

HALL OF AGES
JURASSIC
208–145 MILLION YEARS AGO

Apatosaurus

Brachiosaurus

Stegosaurus

Kentrosaurus

THIS WAY
TO THE
CRETACEOUS
→

Yandusaurus

Compsognathus

15

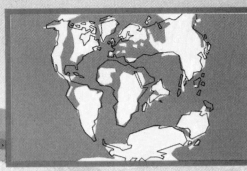

This is how the world looked during the late Cretaceous Period.

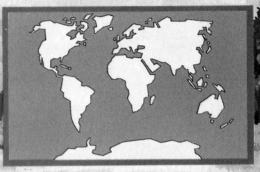

This is how the world looks now.

Pteranodon
(Pterosaur)

Iguanodon

Muttaburrasaurus

Tarbosaurus

Hypsilophodon

You've now entered the last and longest period of the dinosaurs. The climate is now more varied. Plant and animal life is all around. This is the heyday of the dinosaurs. And it's the time when landmasses have split away from one another to form continents. Land has shifted. Mountain ranges are beginning to rise. The land that will be Central America is underwater. Earthquakes, volcanoes, and other natural disasters have pushed the surface of the earth around and created cliffs. Sea floors have been raised. In some places seashells can be found at the tops of mountains!

Dinosaurs can no longer wander freely around the world. They're cut off from one another, and they have evolved in different ways in different places. There are many more dinosaur species. Some animals and plants are evolving that are still around today. Can you find some of them?

Ichthyornis
(Toothed bird)

Shantungosaurus

mbeosaurus

Saltasaurus

Ouranosaurus

Triceratops

Is this all one dinosaur?

HALL OF AGES
CRETACEOUS
145–65 MILLION YEARS AGO

Clue: This dinosaur lived during the early part of the Cretaceous Period.

HALL OF WEIGHTS

Dinosaurs varied tremendously in size. To give you an idea of how big they were, each dinosaur shown here is standing next to a modern animal of a similar size.

As you can see, Brachiosaurus is the largest dinosaur in this hall. But this dinosaur is not the largest dinosaur of all time. So far, the largest dinosaur may be Ultrasaurus, which probably weighed 100 tons and was as tall as a six-story building. The smallest true dinosaur may have been Compsognathus, which was about as big as a chicken.

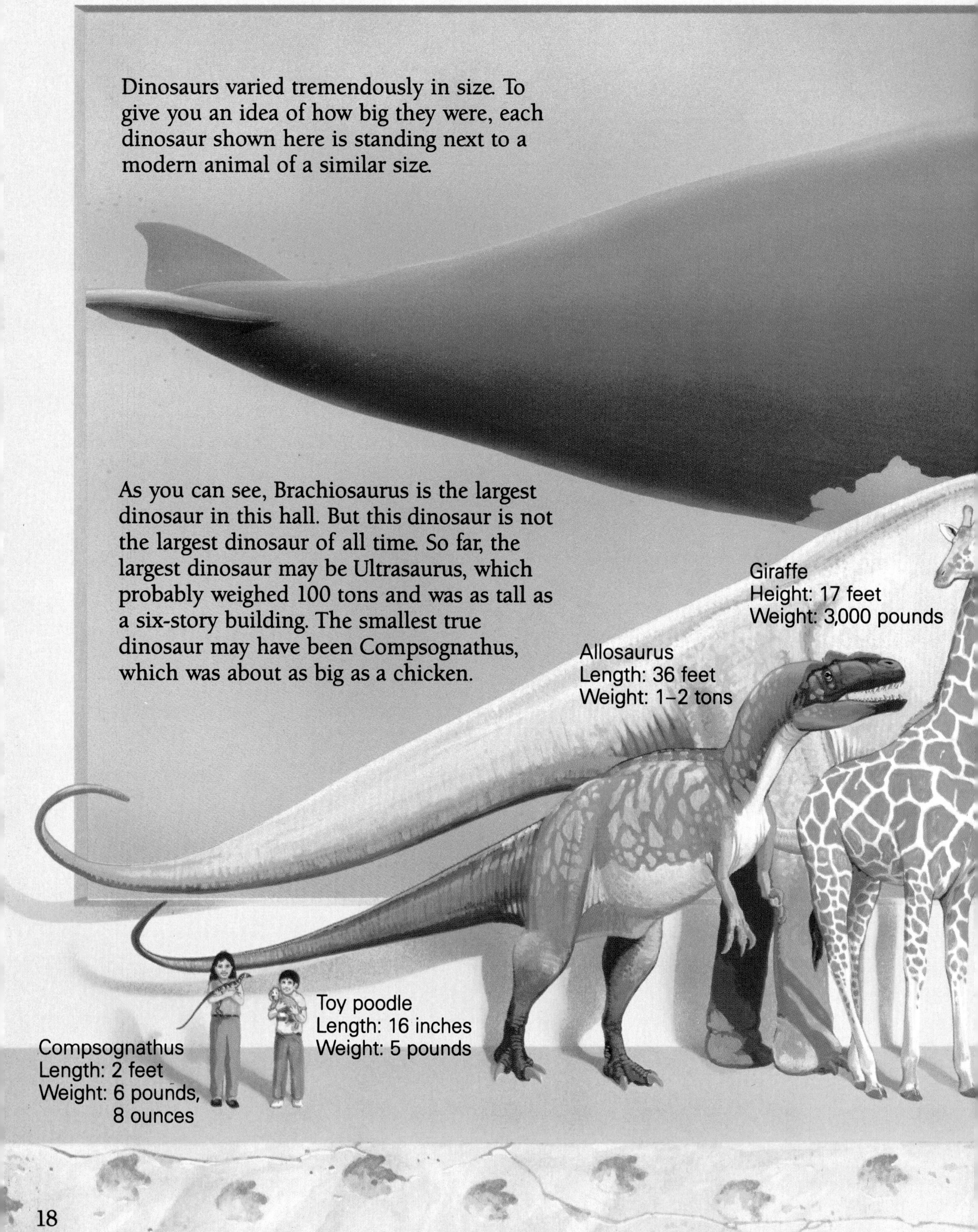

Giraffe
Height: 17 feet
Weight: 3,000 pounds

Allosaurus
Length: 36 feet
Weight: 1–2 tons

Toy poodle
Length: 16 inches
Weight: 5 pounds

Compsognathus
Length: 2 feet
Weight: 6 pounds,
        8 ounces

Brachiosaurus
Length: 75 feet
Weight: 40 tons

Right whale
Length: 60 feet
Weight: 60 tons

African elephant
Height: 11½ feet
Weight: 6½ tons

Tyrannosaurus rex
Length: 39 feet
Height: 18 feet, 6 inches
Weight: 7 tons

Quarter horse
Height: 5 feet
Weight: 1,000 pounds

THIS WAY FOR THE
INSIDE STORY
ON DINOSAURS
→

Camptosaurus
Length: 17 feet
Weight: 1,100 pounds

These tracks measure 30 inches. A large elephant's tracks
are about 20 inches. Would you say these are the tracks
of a large, medium, or small dinosaur?

HALL OF BONES

One way to learn about dinosaurs is by studying their bones. Bones tell a story, if you know what they're saying:

(1) Back bones with thick walls hold up a large body. They tell you that the dinosaur they belonged to was big.

(2) A straight thigh bone with a rounded top that fits into the hip bone shows that the dinosaur walked erect, like a horse.

(3) Long foot bones and high ankles show that many dinosaurs walked on their toes.

(4) Foot bones also tell us that dinosaurs had three, four, or five toes.

Dinosaur experts try to put the bones together to get a picture of the whole animal. Sometimes, of course, they make mistakes!

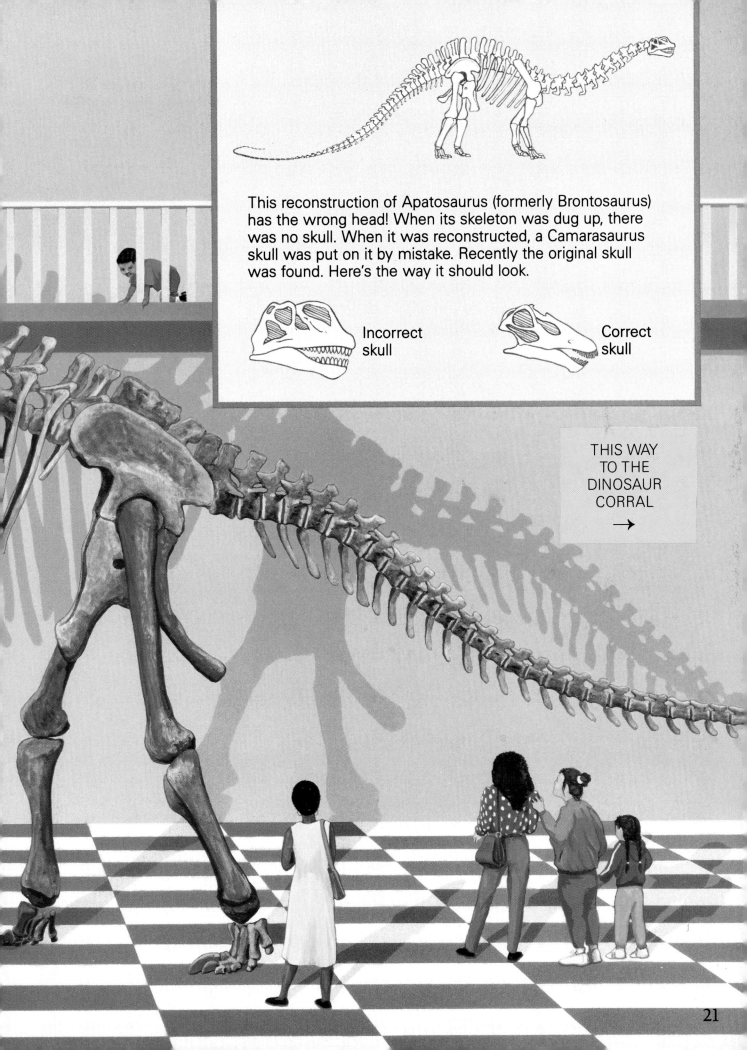

This reconstruction of Apatosaurus (formerly Brontosaurus) has the wrong head! When its skeleton was dug up, there was no skull. When it was reconstructed, a Camarasaurus skull was put on it by mistake. Recently the original skull was found. Here's the way it should look.

Incorrect skull

Correct skull

THIS WAY TO THE DINOSAUR CORRAL
→

DINOSAUR CORRAL

Here we've rounded up some dinosaurs according to kind. Some dinosaur experts say dinosaurs were reptiles. Others say they were ancestors of birds. Both groups agree that there were lizard-hipped dinosaurs (*saurischians*) and bird-hipped dinosaurs (*ornithiscians*).

All saurischians had hip bones that look like this. Note that in saurischians the pubic bone comes forward. All the carnivores (meat-eaters), like Tyrannosaurus rex, come from this group.

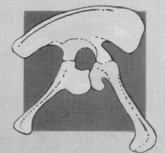

Pubic bone

Brachiosaurus

Diplodocus

Camarasaurus

Omeisaurus

Tyrannosaurus rex

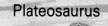

SAURISCHIANS

Plateosaurus

Struthiomimus

Ceratosaurus

Coelophysis

Deinonychus

All ornithiscians had hip bones that look like this. Their pubic bones point backward. Most bird-hipped dinosaurs were herbivores (plant-eaters). A few were probably insect-eaters. Some bird-hipped dinosaurs had bony rods in their tails. This may have been to keep their tails straight and stiff for balance as they walked and ran.

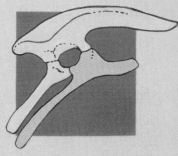

Pubic bone

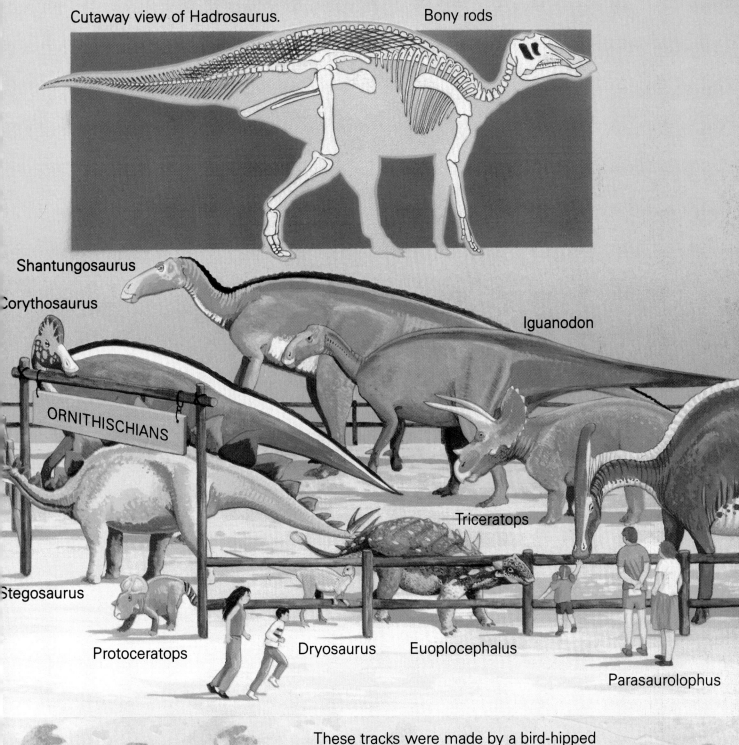

Cutaway view of Hadrosaurus.

Bony rods

Shantungosaurus

Corythosaurus

Iguanodon

ORNITHISCHIANS

Triceratops

Stegosaurus

Protoceratops

Dryosaurus

Euoplocephalus

Parasaurolophus

These tracks were made by a bird-hipped dinosaur. Would you say it was walking on two legs or four?

Many fossil skeletons are found with bones missing. Experts create the whole reconstruction by looking at related skeletons.

Someone was lucky enough to find an almost complete fossil skeleton of a dinosaur in Wyoming. The pieces were brought from the site. Now the experts will try to figure out which dinosaur the bones came from. Then they'll fit the parts together and build a dinosaur skeleton from the bones.

FOSSIL LAB

MYSTERY BONES
FOUND IN WYOMING

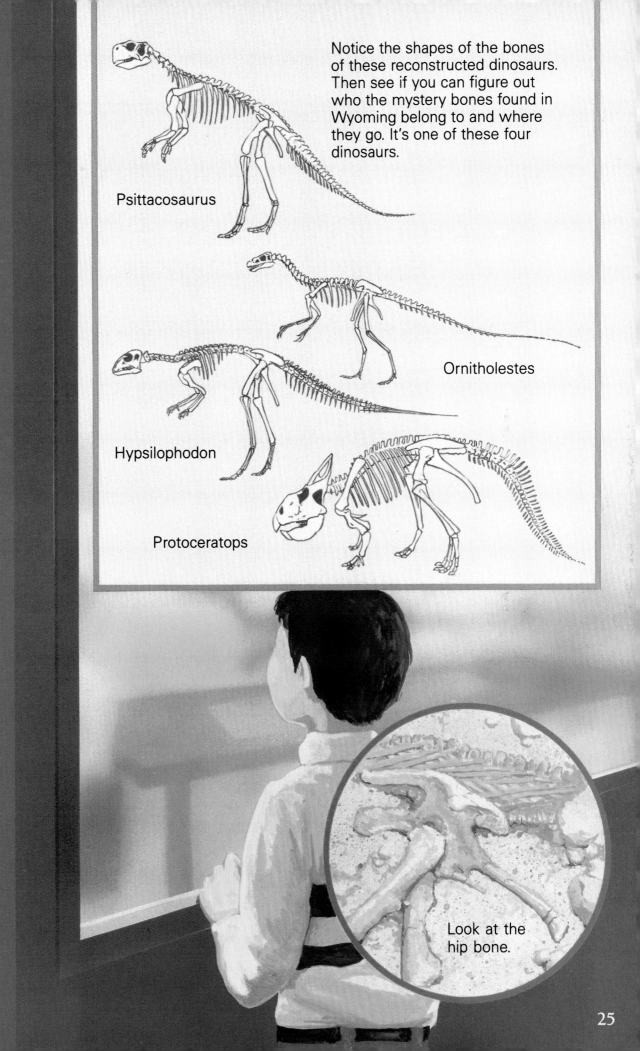

Notice the shapes of the bones of these reconstructed dinosaurs. Then see if you can figure out who the mystery bones found in Wyoming belong to and where they go. It's one of these four dinosaurs.

Psittacosaurus

Ornitholestes

Hypsilophodon

Protoceratops

Look at the hip bone.

The dinosaur experts have figured out that the bones from Wyoming belonged to the small, 6-foot-long dinosaur called Ornitholestes, which means "bird robber." Workers cleaned hardened sand from the skull with sewing needles. Where the bones were broken, they repaired them with glass fiber. Some missing tail bones were made from molds. Pipes were used to support the dinosaur's tail in this position, because scientists think it used the tail for balance when it ran.

Here are three small-scale reconstructions of the dinosaur that made these tracks. The reconstructions were made at different times in history. Only one is correct.

HALL OF HEADS

Jaws and teeth can give you a clue as to what and how the animal ate. From the shape of these teeth and skulls, do you have any ideas about what each of these dinosaurs ate?

Tyrannosaurus rex

Hypsilophodon

Camptosaurus

Ceratosaurus

From a skull you can often figure out the shape of a dinosaur's ears, eyes, and nostrils. You can also see how large its brain was.

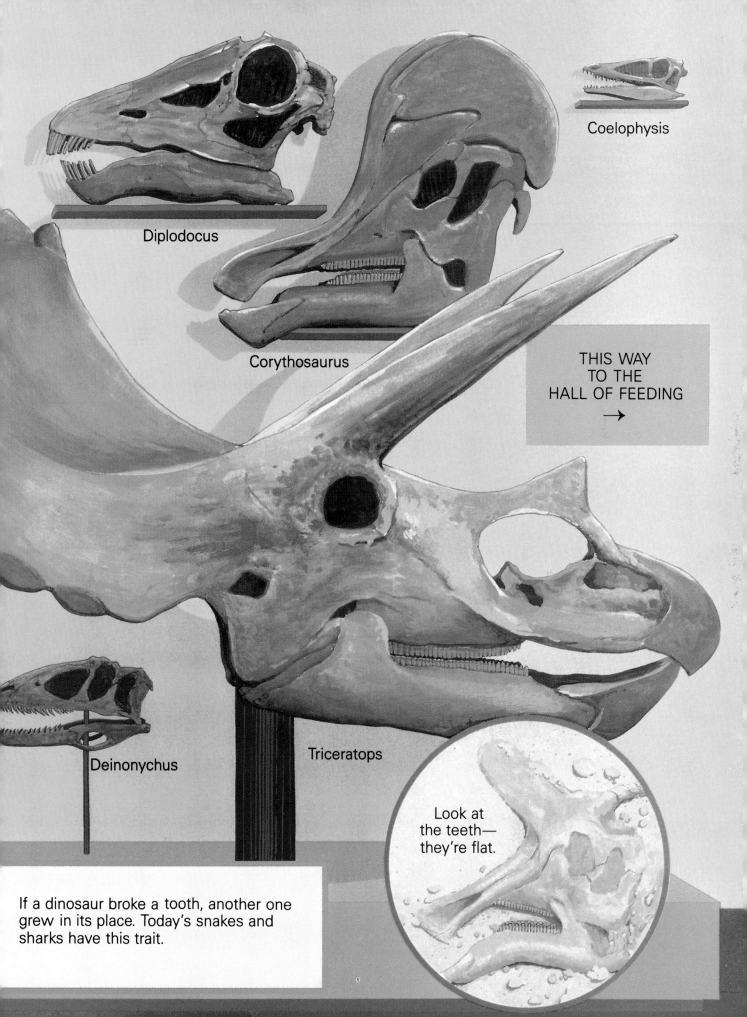

Coelophysis

Diplodocus

Corythosaurus

THIS WAY
TO THE
HALL OF FEEDING
→

Deinonychus

Triceratops

Look at
the teeth—
they're flat.

If a dinosaur broke a tooth, another one
grew in its place. Today's snakes and
sharks have this trait.

Peglike teeth such as these were for browsing and cropping bushes, trees, and plants.

Diplodocus

Carnivores needed knifelike fangs or sawteeth like these to slice through flesh.

Tyrannosaurus rex

HALL OF FEEDING

Some dinosaurs ate only meat. Others ate only plants. The plant-eaters (herbivores) outnumbered the meat-eaters (carnivores). Both herbivores and carnivores were fitted with teeth to eat the kind of food they needed to live on. A single dinosaur tooth can often reveal the time in which that dinosaur lived, as well as its size, its diet, and whether it was a carnivore or an herbivore

Sharpened cheek teeth belonged to herbivores that munched tough twigs and leaves.

Plant-eaters that ate woody plants often had beaks that acted like scissors.

Corythosaurus

Triceratops

Here are the teeth of the mystery dinosaur who made these tracks. Was it a carnivore or an herbivore?

Herbivores had to munch constantly to keep those big bodies going. Some plant-eating dinosaurs grazed on the ground. Others browsed the trees. The shape of a dinosaur's body and its teeth are clues to what it ate and how it got its food. Long-necked herbivores ate from trees. Those built low to the ground or with S-shaped necks were browsers and grazers.

Diplodocus

Camptosaurus

Coelophysis

Carnivores did not have to eat as often as herbivores. But carnivores had to chase down their meal. Meat-eaters had claws to help hold or kill prey. Their teeth, set in those powerful jaws, finished the job.

Look what's happening. The carnivores are attacking the herbivores. To save the herbivores, which dinosaurs would you remove?

Lambeosaurus

Ceratosaurus

Deinonychus

Tenontosaurus

Hypsilophodon

Stones called gastroliths are sometimes found around the stomach area of fossilized plant-eaters. This may mean that some dinosaurs swallowed stones to help grind up their food, as chickens and ostriches do today.

HALL OF ARMOR

Plant-eating dinosaurs had ways to protect themselves from being dinner for a carnivore. Some traveled in group or herds, like modern-day elephants. And most of them had some form of armor—body plates; spikes; spines; neck frills; or huge, tough scales.

If a meat-eater got too close, Euoplocephalus used its tail like a club.

Clue: This dinosaur did *not* have heavy armor.

Triceratops' skin was tough as leather, and it had a large neck frill and spikes to protect its head.

Most armored dinosaurs belonged to three groups: ankylosaurs, ceratopsians, and stegosaurs. Here are dinosaurs from each of these groups. Can you match them with their relatives in the Hall of Armor?

Scelidosaurus did not belong to any of these groups. Its armor tells us that it may have been an ancestor of two of the groups.

Styracosaurus
(Ceratopsian)

Kentrosaurus
(Stegosaur)

Edmontonia
(Ankylosaur)

Monoclonius
(Ceratopsian)

Pinacosaurus
(Ankylosaur)

Huayangosaurus
(Stegosaur)

When these armored dinosaurs lived

	Ankylosaurs	Cerotopsians	Stegosaurs
Cretaceous			
Jurassic			
Triassic			

Stegosaurus had huge, bony plates along its spine and spikes along its tail. It could lash out with a tail that may have been as much as 10 feet long.

Not all dinosaurs wore armor. Some must have had other ways to disappear into the landscape. Here's a group of dinosaurs wearing natural camouflage. There are three dinosaurs whose colors blend in so well that you can hardly see them. Or can you?

Kritosaurus   Yandusaurus

The dinosaur that made these tracks had spikes on its front feet.

Here's a piece of
fossilized skin.

Massospondylus

DINOSAUR NURSERY

An egg holds everything a baby creature needs to grow on. Early in the history of life on earth, fish, insects, and reptiles began to be hatched from eggs. These eggs all had soft shells, so they were easily broken or washed away. After a long time, reptiles began to lay hard-shelled eggs. Those eggs were a safer place for developing young.

Fossils of dinosaur eggs began to be found in the 1920s. We know they were hard-shelled eggs because soft-shelled eggs would have rotted away. Scientists now believe that many dinosaurs laid eggs. It's possible, however, that some dinosaurs may have borne live young, like mammals do.

Oviraptor is hanging around because it eats eggs.

Oviraptor

Here are some different kinds of eggs with hard shells. (Lengths are in inches.)

Alligator
← 3 →

Maiasaura
← 8 →

Hypselosaurus
← 10 →

Chicken
$2 \frac{3}{4}$

Pond slider turtle
$1 \frac{3}{8}$

Mussaurus
1

Orodromeus
← $6 \frac{3}{4}$ →

Protoceratops
← 8 →

Maiasaura is an herbivore, so she is bringing leaves and fruit to the nest for the babies to eat.

The sandy rim of this nest may mean that Maiasaura scooped out a place and brooded her eggs by sitting *over* them. The rim would have kept her from sitting *on* the eggs, which would have destroyed them.

Some dinosaurs laid their eggs in long trails, as if they were moving along as they laid them.

Maiasaura

Fossils of young hatchlings were found in the maiasaur's nest. This means that the mother must have brought food for the babies. In species such as Orodromeus, where the mother doesn't care for the young, the babies leave the nest right after they're born.

Orodromeus

Protoceratops

THIS WAY TO THE FLIGHT CHAMBER
→

The large number of eggs found in this nest makes it likely that more than one Protoceratops laid them. These dinosaurs may have lived together in family groups and laid their eggs in one big nest.

Quetzalcoatlus
Wingspan: 32 feet

Pterodactylus
Wingspan: 2 feet

Rhamphorhynchus
Wingspan: 6 $\frac{1}{2}$ feet

FLIGHT CHAMBER

These tracks were *not*
made by a flying reptile.

Dimorphodon
Wingspan: 4 1/2 feet

Pteranodon
Wingspan: 4 feet

It's a clear Mesozoic evening. The pterosaurs are hunting insects in the air the way chimney swifts, swallows, and other birds and bats do today. Were the pterosaurs the ancestors of today's birds?

Pterosaurs had wings—webs of skin that seemed to grow out of the fourth finger on their front claws. They glided and soared through the air. But pterosaurs were reptiles, not dinosaurs.

Crow-sized Archaeopteryx probably didn't fly very well, but it had feathers. That's why many scientists think that it was the first bird.

This is a single track, but there's evidence that these particular dinosaurs may also have traveled in herds.

CAVE OF WONDERS

Diplodocus is the longest dinosaur discovered so far. It was 90 feet long and had bony skids under its tail that protected the tail when it was dragged on the ground.

Baryonyx had crocodile jaws and a huge claw on each hand. It ate fish.

Parasaurolophus had a large head crest. What was it for? Scientists think that this dinosaur may have made trumpeting sounds through this hornlike crest.

Are you still in the dark about who these tracks belong to? It's the track of Iguanodon, whose name means "iguana tooth." Iguanodon was a plant-eating dinosaur about 33 feet long that weighed between two and four tons.

Pachycephalosaurus had a bony dome 10 inches thick on its head. Its skull was 2 feet long.

The smallest dinosaur skeleton ever found belongs to Mussaurus. It's only 8 inches long and was probably a baby.

Ultrasaurus had a shoulder bone 9 feet long. It must have weighed 100 tons, as much as 200 cows, and was as tall as a six-story building.

Stegosaurus had armor plates on its back that probably acted like cooling fans.

THIS WAY TO THE HALL OF FAME

Here is the entire dinosaur fossil uncovered.

It's Lambeosaurus.

At least three important dinosaur discoveries have been made by young people.

William Smith never went to school. But he taught himself to make maps. And he kept his eyes open. One day almost two hundred years ago he was mapping a coal mine when he noticed the layers of earth (*strata*) in the mine. He noticed that each layer seemed to have its own kind of fossils. He went all over England checking strata. After a while people began to call him "Strata" Smith. His finding—that strata provide a way to "read" the history of earth—helped scientists to learn about the animals that lived at various times.

William Smith

Professor Edward Hitchcock could never have done his work cataloging ancient birdlike tracks if it hadn't been for a young farm boy named Pliny Moody. One day in 1802 Pliny discovered a set of gigantic footprints in a field in South Hadley, Massachusetts. Edward Hitchcock was sure they were the tracks of ancient birds. In fact, they were the tracks of early dinosaurs.

Pliny Moody

HALL OF FAME

In 1811, eleven-year-old Mary Anning was was walking near her parents' shell shop in Lyme Regis, England, when she discovered a fossil skeleton in a limestone cliff. It was an ichthyosaur, a sea reptile that lived at the same time as the dinosaurs. Mary later found other specimens. Scientists came from all over the world to see her fossil collection. There is some evidence that the tongue-twister "She sells seashells by the seashore" was about Mary Anning!

Mary Anning

e first to scover fossil eth and bones Iguanodon 822).

Gideon Mantell
Mary Mantell

The first scientist to state, correctly, that certain dinosaurs walked on two legs (1858).

Joseph Leidy

He is one of the scientists who believe that the dinosaurs were warm-blooded.

Robert Bakker

In 1971 he found bones of a massive dinosaur that he named Supersaurus.

James Jensen

The scientist who discovered that at least one kind of dinosaur cared for its young at the nest.

John R. Horner

Dinosaur Index

PAGES	NAME	ORDER (Saurischian or Ornithischian)	LOCATION (Where found)	PERIOD (When it lived)
10–11	Albertosaurus (al-BERT-oh-sawr-us)	S	U.S.A. (Montana), Canada	Late Cretaceous
10–11, 14–15, 18–19	Allosaurus (AL-oh-sawr-us)	S	U.S.A. (Colorado, Wyoming, Utah), Tanzania, Australia	Late Jurassic
10–11	Anchisaurus (AN-kee-sawr-us)	S	U.S.A. (Connecticut, Arizona), Germany, South Africa	Early Jurassic
10–11, 14–15, 20–21	Apatosaurus (a-PAT-oh-sawr-us)	S	U.S.A. (Colorado, Utah, Wyoming, Oklahoma)	Late Jurassic
42–43	Baryonyx (bar-ee-ON-ics)	S	England	Early Cretaceous
10–11, 14–15, 18–19, 22–23	Brachiosaurus (BRAK-ee-oh-sawr-us)	S	U.S.A. (Colorado), Portugal, Tanzania	Late Jurassic
22–23	Camarasaurus (kam-AR-ah-sawr-us)	S	U.S.A. (Colorado, Wyoming, Utah, Oklahoma), Portugal	Late Jurassic
10–11, 18–19, 28–29, 32–33	Camptosaurus (KAMP-toh-sawr-us)	O	U.S.A. (Colorado, South Dakota, Utah, Wyoming), Portugal, England	Late Jurassic
10–11, 22–23, 28–29, 32–33	Ceratosaurus (SER-a-toh-sawr-us)	S	U.S.A. (Colorado, Wyoming), Tanzania	Late Jurassic
10–13, 22–23, 28–29, 32–33	Coelophysis (SEE-loh-FY-sis)	S	U.S.A. (Connecticut, New Mexico)	Late Triassic
14–15, 18–19	Compsognathus (KOMP-so-nath-us)	S	Germany, France	Late Jurassic
22–23, 28–31	Corythosaurus (ko-RITH-oh-sawr-us)	O	U.S.A. (Montana), Canada	Late Cretaceous
10–11, 22–23, 28–29, 32–33	Deinonychus (DIE-noh-nik-us)	S	U.S.A. (Montana)	Early Cretaceous
10–11	Dilophosaurus (DIE-lo-foh-sawr-us)	S	U.S.A. (Arizona)	Early Jurassic
14–15, 22–23, 28–29, 30–33, 42–43	Diplodocus (dip-LOD-oh-kus)	S	U.S.A. (Colorado, Utah, Wyoming)	Late Jurassic
22–23	Dryosaurus (DRY-oh-sawr-us)	O	U.S.A. (Colorado, Utah, Wyoming), Tanzania	Late Jurassic
34–35	Edmontonia (ed-mont-OH-nee-ah)	O	U.S.A. (Montana)	Late Cretaceous
10–11, 22–23, 34–35	Euoplocephalus (yu-op-loh-SEF-a-lus)	O	Canada	Late Cretaceous
10–11	Hadrosaurus (HAD-roh-sawr-us)	O	U.S.A. (South Dakota, Montana, New Jersey, New Mexico)	Late Cretaceous
34–35	Huayangosaurus (hwah-YANG-oh-sawr-us)	O	China	Middle Jurassic
16–17, 24–25, 28–29, 32–33	Hypsilophodon (HIP-sel-oh-fo-don)	O	U.S.A. (South Dakota), England, Portugal	Early Cretaceous
16–17, 22–23, 42–43	Iguanodon (ig-WAN-oh-don)	O	U.S.A. (Utah), Germany, Spain, Mongolia, Belgium, England	Early Cretaceous
10–11, 14–15, 34–35	Kentrosaurus (KENT-roh-sawr-us)	O	Tanzania	Late Jurassic
36–37	Kritosaurus (KRI-toh-sawr-us)	O	U.S.A. (Montana, New Mexico), Canada	Late Cretaceous

PAGES	NAME	ORDER (Saurischian or Ornithischian)	LOCATION (Where found)	PERIOD (When it lived)
10–11, 16–17, 32–33, 42–43	Lambeosaurus (LAM-bee-oh-sawr-us)	O	U.S.A. (California, Montana), Canada	Late Cretaceous
10–11	Lesothosaurus (leh-SOH-toh-sawr-us)	O	Lesotho	Early Jurassic
38–39	Maiasaura (MY-ah-sawr-ah)	O	U.S.A. (Montana)	Late Cretaceous
10–11, 36–37	Massospondylus (MASS-oh-spon-dih-lus)	S	U.S.A. (Arizona), South Africa, Lesotho, Zimbabwe	Early Jurassic
34–35	Monoclonius (MON-oh-klo-nee-us)	O	U.S.A. (Montana), Canada	Late Cretaceous
38–39, 42–43	Mussasaurus (muss-ah-sawr-us)	S	Argentina	Late Triassic
16–17	Muttaburrasaurus (moot-a-BUR-a-sawr-us)	O	Australia	Early Cretaceous
22–23	Omeisaurus (O-may-ee-sawr-us)	S	China	Late Jurassic
24–27	Ornitholestes (or-nith-oh-LES-teez)	S	U.S.A. (Wyoming, Utah)	Late Jurassic
10–11	Ornithomimus (or-nith-oh-MY-muss)	S	U.S.A. (Colorado, Montana), Canada, Tibet	Late Cretaceous
38–39	Orodromeus (or-oh-DROM-ee-us)	O	U.S.A. (Montana)	Late Cretaceous
16–17	Ouranosaurus (oo-RAN-oh-sawr-us)	O	Niger	Early Cretaceous
38–39	Oviraptor (oh-vi-RAPT-or)	S	China, Mongolia	Late Cretaceous
42–43	Pachycephalosaurus (PAK-ee-KEF-al-oh-sawr-us)	O	U.S.A. (Wyoming), Canada	Late Cretaceous
22–23, 42–43	Parasaurolophus (par-ah-SAWR-oh-lo-fus)	O	U.S.A. (New Mexico, Utah), Canada	Late Cretaceous
34–35	Pinacosaurus (pin-ak-oh-sawr-us)	O	China, Mongolia	Late Cretaceous
10–11	Pisanosaurus (pee-SAN-oh-sawr-us)	O	Argentina	Late Triassic
10–13, 22–23	Plateosaurus (PLAY-tee-oh-sawr-us)	S	France, Germany, Switzerland	Late Triassic
22–25, 38–39	Protoceratops (pro-toh-SER-a-tops)	O	China, Mongolia, U.S.S.R.	Late Cretaceous
24–25	Psittacosaurus (si-TAK-oh-sawr-us)	O	China, Mongolia, U.S.S.R.	Early Cretaceous
10–11, 16–17	Saltasaurus (SALT-a-sawr-us)	S	Argentina	Late Cretaceous
10–11	Scelidosaurus (skel-ide-oh-sawr-us)	O	England	Early Jurassic
10–11, 16–17, 22–23	Shantungosaurus (shan-TUNG-oh-sawr-us)	O	China	Late Cretaceous
10–11, 14–15, 22–23, 34–35, 42–43	Stegosaurus (STEG-oh-sawr-us)	O	U.S.A. (Colorado, Utah, Oklahoma, Wyoming)	Late Jurassic

PAGES	NAME	ORDER (Saurischian or Ornithischian)	LOCATION (Where found)	PERIOD (When it lived)
22–23	Struthiomimus (STROOTH-ee-oh-mime-us)	S	U.S.A. (New Jersey), Canada	Late Cretaceous
10–11, 34–35	Styracosaurus (STY-rak-oh-sawr-us)	O	U.S.A. (Montana), Canada	Late Cretaceous
16–17	Tarbosaurus (TARB-oh-sawr-us)	S	China, Mongolia	Late Cretaceous
10–11, 32–33	Tenontosaurus (ten-ON-toh-sawr-us)	O	U.S.A. (Arizona, Montana, Oklahoma, Texas)	Early Cretaceous
10–11, 16–17, 22–23, 28–31, 34–35	Triceratops (try-SER-ah-tops)	O	U.S.A. (Montana, Colorado, South Dakota, Wyoming), Canada	Late Cretaceous
10–11, 18–19, 22–23, 28–31	Tyrannosaurus rex (ty-RAN-oh-sawr-us recs)	S	U.S.A. (Montana, Texas, Wyoming), Mongolia, Canada	Late Cretaceous
42–43	Ultrasaurus (UL-tra-sawr-us)	S	U.S.A. (Colorado)	Late Jurassic
14–15, 36–37	Yandusaurus (yan-doo-sawr-us)	O	China	Middle Jurassic

About the Contributors

Barbara Brenner, the author, is a writer, editor, teacher, and consultant on educational projects. Most recently, she has been senior editor in the Publications Division of the Bank Street College of Education. Ms. Brenner has written more than fifty books for children, including many on natural science for which she has won numerous awards. She has five times received the Outstanding Science Book award given by the National Science Teachers Association and the Children's Book Council. One of her books, *On the Frontier with Mr. Audubon,* was selected by *School Library Journal* as "The Best of the Best" among the books published for children over twenty-six publishing seasons.

Donna Braginetz, the illustrator, graduated from Colorado State University with a B.A. in art education and a special interest in paleontological illustration. Ms. Braginetz contributes regular features to natural history magazines, including *Natural History,* published by the American Museum of Natural History,

and *Ranger Rick,* a magazine for children published by the National Wildlife Federation. She has drawn reconstructions of fossil mammals for the Denver Museum of Natural History and has recently illustrated a forthcoming book for adults, *Colorado's Dinosaur Story.* This is her second book for children.

Dr. Peter Dodson, the science consultant, studied paleontology at Yale University and has three degrees in geology. He is now an associate professor of animal biology and a teacher of veterinary anatomy at the University of Pennsylvania Veterinary School. He is also a research associate at the Academy of Natural Sciences museum in Philadelphia. Dr. Dodson writes for both children and adults and has more than fifty publications to his credit. He was coauthor of two children's books, *Baby Dinosaurs* and *Giant Dinosaurs* which were praised in the *New York Times Book Review.* His notable books for adults include *The Dinosaurs,* for which he was consultant, and *The Dinosauria,* a scholarly work that he coedited.